THRESHOLDS

THRESHOLDS

An anthology of poems
by Red Door Poets

Clayhanger Press

First Printing 2022

Published by Clayhanger Press
Newcastle under Lyme
Staffordshire
www.clayhangerpress.co.uk

ISBN 978-1-7391770-0-3

Contents

Hotel

Ranks of doors, through which
lives pass like birth, stand
at attention along corridors.

A door is a wall that moves.
Beyond lies last night's air
and walls falling mote by mote.

You may replace a door
but not the void
a door unmasks.

In the locked room nothing happens,
though when you enter
the clock has combed its face.

The moon inspects a keyhole,
a silver eye no one can see
glows in the mirror.

When the door is opened
a fridge of light breaks on the floor
and soaks the carpet.

The front door is locked at ten.
Use your key to enter.
The bar will not be open.

Before you go you must wait
while the debt that will follow
across every shuttered threshold

is written down,
and your ghost is cleaned
from the room you left.

Chris Hardy   **9**

Meibion Glyndwr
The Sons of Glyndwr

It was when they were burning houses.
We hoped they wouldn't notice if we
bought an old cottage in fields
where Tommy Edwards kept his hens.
Rats' nests beneath the floor,
no electric, water, phone,
damp lime plaster, cracked flags
seeping rain, a huge plank door
through which the sun cut
blades of light at dawn.

Standing by the gate at the end of the track
I gave Tommy a block of red bank notes.
He thumbed it through then handed back
a wedge, *luck money* he said,
to ward off the curse that might fall
on him for selling, or us for buying
a few of earth's own acres.

Though I could drive a tractor
I could not deliver a calf,
milk a herd, mind a bull,
gather sheep from Giant's Grave,
throw fifty bales from a trailer
into the hayloft before supper,
so it was back to town for work,
but what to do with the land?

At Abbey Cwmhir, where the prince
lies beneath a black stone sword
and dark conifers crowd down hillsides
above the monks' fishponds,
an old man outside the Happy Union,
wearing leather gaiters, flannel waistcoat
and a hedging gauntlet,
who'd been up to Mametz

Chris Hardy

with the fusiliers, called over his
burnt brown, long-haired son,
who said he'd cut our grass
but if we were late to pay
he'd torch our barn and kill us,
which seemed a bargain at the time.

The little house acquired lintels, purlins,
a coat of render, paint, a nailed cascade
of sharp black slates flowing down the pitch.
When we returned after months away
and lit coal in the grate,
tears ran down its cold stone walls
as we opened eyelid curtains
to see outside a new laid hedge
and silent mown meadows.

Chris Hardy

Theotokos

God-bearer imprisoned in the dark
except when a shining blade
slides beneath the lintel.
Opening the cracked blue door
the sun's breath fills her cell,
gold air enshrines her face.

Confined so she cannot escape
from those who pray to her for help,
fearing the father who sacrificed his son
to teach us all a lesson.
Her eyes are patient,
her milk will always run.

Tick of a match, a candle flares
for a friend left lying in a room,
who feels a breeze part curtains
to admit the day and also
shadows, which light kills
as they try to run away.

Chris Hardy

Remember how you slipped on my cities?

I map countries – shaded areas are land; the rest is sea.
The sun streams in a wide strait between my feet
and the table by the door. I place marbles as cities,
bottle caps as boats, never look at the door –

nicotine-tarred paint, flaked along the top,
the spy hole too high up without a chair.
I hear the street door open, a pause, shut,
light footsteps run up, then vanish.

I name the countries – like at school
where Miss Sterup, tapping with her rod
on the pull-down map of Europe, had us chant –
Our neighbours are Germany, Sweden, Norway.

Scandinavia consists of three countries.
Germany is divided into two halves by a wall.
Great Britain consists of three countries.
Her world was crawling with war –*The War*

– as if it had just ended, her fear staining us.
No. This floor is mine – Øresund, and here my city.
I position marbles in a neat, red and white
spiral for Copenhagen. Yellow and blue – Stockholm.

The sun sets. Lines between sea and land soften.
Borders dissolve and Norway, Sweden, Denmark are lost,
all of Europe landlocked –
                                        one terrified shadow.

Hanne Busck-Nielsen   **13**

Every beast is here

        Heads, claws, horns and fins
whip of a tail – mesh of life
of leaves and petals
            and the dead.
Oh, look –

        *

A mouth   and another   and there
here   lips lifting

                          lowering
teeth clicking   tongues ripped loose
root to tip   mouths spit   splutter

growl   mutter   the wood
panels heave   the door is   locked
and all

               is absence   each one
a completion a creature   a howl

while time turns
            inside the lock its iron beat

        *

Outside, late May.
        The yellow rose. A breeze
through clothes on the line.
           Shade under the tree
and, like a bullock ruminating
in the long grass, Death is bored, sleepy.

Half-light

We become shadows –
            slipping on mud and flat stones.
    Water blinks amongst tufts of mossy grass
– a trickle of voices
            underfoot in the squelch.

    Spruce and ochre larch
dim to silhouettes
            against the sloping sky
lowest branches layering with mist –
                elverkongen's døtre dance.

    Clod-clowning troll *Bobbarækus* rumbles.
I am a disappeared child –
            six revelling *elver*-girls encircle me
                their tree-rot hollow backs sway.

The moon is impartial –
            a freezing glare
                but a lost line remembers itself
        –

Aldrig ræd for mørkets magt
Never dread the might of darkness –

            guides us through bracken and heather
until at last we are back on a road curving the fell
            dumb to dark, night eating silence
                and no owl or wind to make us real.

Aldrig ræd for mørkets magt is a line from a Danish
hymn by Chr. Richardt, 1867.

.

Hanne Busck-Nielsen   **15**

Something completely else came in

Is that what she said or was she talking
about the fear of flying?

The broom had saved her – she flew on it
from the edge of the cliff;

there was a room with many views
in the house where she landed;

she quickly covered every pane
every twinkle of light

with the shadows of her terrors –
a rainbow of spaces began to appear –

some were loud and clear, others dark,
darker than the bottom of the sea;

some had strange creatures – eerie
anglerfish, vampire squid, spaghetti

monster, ghost fish; some were a cluster
of young stars flaring to life –

she thought she'd stay;
she thought she'll be safe.

Beatriz Echeverri

Towards High Barnet

She was asleep or just
resting her eyes –
tunnelling them.

Her boots – worn out –
dirtied on some muddy path.

An inside-out coat
– also worn out –
covered her knees;

it tagged along with
her dreams sweet or sour.

The brakes' squeals and squeaks,
the piercing rolling of metal on metal,
the stops and announcements – lure her along.

Mind the gap, mind the gap,
at the next station the last doors will not open.

Beatriz Echeverri   17

Listen carefully

the cow was having a chat with the fish
– by the fish tank –
the screwdriver hadn't worked its magic

they wanted to isolate a bit of the tank
– to allow the cow in
closer to the fish

the lilies were floppy
and the view to the sea was blocked

it was too dark
when i grow up – the fish said –
i'll leave this tank

i'll live free in one of those calm ponds
nearer the sea

and i'll build a shed
for you – dear cow –
to come and visit

it'll be an open shed – only
you could lock it if you wished –

after you left

the skies were so huge   milky blue
all darkness banished by the near imperative
to let there be light always

that morning a crow stood on the tv aerial in the yard
as if it might catch the news while I waited
knowing there's not anything new in any of this

we have only sky and tree   the old signs
of bird shadow on the horizon   the way
the branches shake as if evening will explode
from darkness drawn up from their roots
the wild heat that forms gems
the earth's core   gold forged in the crush
of supernovae   neutron stars

all that day the sky was wide open
as if it would be easy to pass in and forget
there are no realms of light after sunset

the colours separated and merged
as if not quite ready for the impossible
one-way ticket to the dark
though we know how the day will end
how the earth waits   water   leaf   rock

I don't know how light dies
but after you left the evening spread out
in blue swathes beneath lava
the sky always burning
and that night the last clouds flew off like dark geese

The Reflecting Pool

You outstrip me
touch my skin and green bursts from my fingers
when I call out.
Now I am nothing but the tiny leaves that rustle
with the pulse of my fear.
A plane drones overhead like a searchlight
and even the water trembles.
The slightest vibration changes my shape,
but you would even chase my reflection
gather yourself and leap,
cry out the way you always do
at this moment when you think you have me,
pause, mid-air, untouched by water that's a dream
of night where a moon glides on a loop,
splits chiaroscuro green,
marks time, concentric, melting to an edge.

Lesley Sharpe

arguments against sun

come with me to the lakes you said
      even if it only rains
            rain like love

seals time   prepares us   rinses us clean
      as an eggshell or salt
            traps us indoors

or out   my umbrella opens like a purple crocus
      invites divination by street lamp
            of the rain's voice

reads its shifting light   a thousand wet moths
      that hover at its edges
            fall into dark

there is always the exhilaration of rain
      that proves itself in clothes
            flattened to flesh

rain with its rush   that shut us in the house
      the downpour   that we folded
            into streams

cul de sac

put the room in a box
craft it some wings
open the window
let it go

ﮩﮩ

Tomorrow

Tonight
all the early stars
have brought out
their sisters – buddies.

Come out, they say.
Look down.
The earth is so dark.
Not a light.

Tom Cunliffe

Remains .... Srebrenica

Thoughts are licking,
niggling flame-like, scattering
as words on a page, birds from scrub, or
seismic lines across the human brow,
web-like, grotesque.

Mind
Winter's minds.
He loved his own children,
was swamped in their embrace
and smiles....
Opening a door,
it licks, niggles.

Time has its own alchemy,
etches a distinct richness –
things worm, decay
but never disappear.
Nothing traps the abundance of seeds
seeping.
The absence of the mouth
does not diminish sound.
Handless, they are not bound.
Truth opens doors,
every door,
it licks,
niggles,
has its own
skeletal chemistry.

Postcard

An orchard of clouds
drew her from the chair,
where for some time,
mother of all bitterness,
she stood looking out, before
grabbing her fur,
left,
clean as an eye following light,
wordless through the door
towards a night of wandering men.

An asylum of hymns,
she returned wailing.
Then, just like that moment before sunset,
or immediately after the blast of a hunter's gun,
when flocks quieten, she settled.
I struggled putting up the Christmas lights,
she stood holding the ladder, looking out into the sun
as if her mind were skimming stones –
her whole sky incomplete.

Tom Cunliffe

Buckingham Palace

The last time my father had a hypo – that time
we thought he was just a bit weary so we left him
to sleep, but when I came back I found him
breathing heavily, he couldn't focus on me (although
he knew who I was, which was a relief); that time
when I called 999 because he was possibly having a stroke
and I spent an age telling the emergency operator
what his symptoms were, and yes, he could lift his arm,
and no, his face was not collapsed, but he didn't seem
to see me now, and he was starting to thrash about
insofar as a very old man with weak legs can thrash,
like a groaning waterwheel turning with heavy,
inevitable churn; and the emergency operator
said she would send an ambulance, which didn't come,
so I rang again and we worked through the same questions
and all the answers this time were more frightening

and I asked where the ambulance was and she said
on its way, and it didn't come, so when I rang the third time,
by which time he was out of it, really out of it, she told me
an ambulance really *was* coming and *two* ambulances arrived
– and they all greeted each other, those paramedics, old
friends, perching like greenfinches round the bedroom,
completing paper-work, taking my father's pulse, assessing
his reactions, at last administering glucose so his breathing
eased back to normal – that's the time I mean; next day,
my father told me he had dreamt that he was walking
up to the front door of Buckingham Palace, so forbidding
yet glorious! but a footman with a kindly manner told him he
could not enter. My father was disappointed, indeed
devastated, but he knew, he said, the footman was right.

Cage

I'll climb up, get in with you, if I may.
There's not much room but squeezed-up is okay –
if you could shift your haunches to the left
and pull your front paws back under your chest.
Yes, squash yourself against the wire grid.
Thank you so much. I'll take these off, get rid
of tee-shirt, hoodie down behind your tail
and tuck my jeans under your water bowl,
push scrunched-up pants and socks between the bars.
It's cold, this concrete cell, under the stars.
I'm shivery and tired but still no tears.
No one's going to look for me in here,
at least, no one I care about. Please curl
around me. Teach me how to howl.

The Choicest Fruit

When I discovered the new door
I went straight in and found
an orchard. I recognised many
of the trees from our garden –
my favourite eater, James Grieve,
laden with smooth striped fruit;
the Bramley by the sloping path,
great green dimples; the crooked
Red Worcester, long dead I'd thought,
bowed by its dew-touched load.

The damson tree from Tysoe
was dark with bantam plums;
the stunted pear (a Conference),
studded with white flowers
which also splashed the grass;
sloes from Henley Down leaning,
offering misty blueblack marbles.

Beside the fallen shed, the bullace
sheltered yellow windfall;
while Dad's last tree, the Orange Pippin,
stood stalwart beyond the Golden
Hornet crab, whose fruit dazzles,
miniature multiplied suns.

Behind all these a new tree. A cherry
fresh-planted, no grass grown over
the roots yet already in full fruit. I pull
down a branch, choose the ripest jewel.
Swallow it, stone and all.

Elizabeth Horsley   27

that art thou

through a singularity in the sky
you move ahead of me

this is the flattest land
the hiss of grass

an arc of radiance
over invisible sea

colours uncoil in swathes
and bolts of brilliance

I drag the rainbow
heavy behind me

the spectrum unsplits
light everywhere

Tat tvam asi (that art thou) is one of the *Mahāvākyas*
(Grand Pronouncements) in Vedantic Hinduism.

Gillie Robic

The Path to the Lake

I used to be a door, knocked upon, kicked open,
slammed shut.

I was handsome, well-built,
my coping stones superbly dressed.

Now my paint is peeling,
I warp into distortion.

I am open, but my rusted lock
complicates the need for a key.

If you stand on this toe-hold where you crack my space,
I may let you through to the choked-up path.

If you find your way back, will you knock, kick me open?
If I slam in your face, which of us will be lost?

dilation

when the sky was clear and the others asleep
she scaled the wardrobe
to reach the skylight
observe the depths and fires of the sky
the swirls and comets
pinpricks and spirals
expanding
irresistible space

she swung over the sill
disembarked

Gillie Robic

Yesterday evening like putrefied grain

a disembodied bulletin
stank the air.

Same old story about profit/greed,
delivered by a mouth in a suit,

reminded me of all put-up jobs.
How we're in thrall

to karaoke kids in the bar
mangling the words of others.

Tell me we're still
enfants terribles.

That even as the earth tires
we're on to something

if we put an earpiece to our drinks
to catch the crunch of ice.

But it all kicks off. The publican
strong-arms us. We comply,

dumb as Adam. He too
was marched off the premises.

Arrival – a gutsy business

and nothing to bring
except the wail of the world.

To set foot –
squeezed, pummelled,
then weighed and tagged.

Lights flicker uncertain.
My newborn cries.
In embarrassment?
So this is the mother.

So this is the child.
Incontrovertible.

Skin smelling
of home.

I am
rearranged.

How –
from my body alone –
to feed,
to ensure a baby
an entire night?

Our see-saw.
I give my clumsiness.
My infant gives
a credulous mouth.

Best put hands over ears not to hear
what will be sworn and promised.

Katie Griffiths

Best not to know,
little one here with me
in the darkness, our beginning.

Door-Botherer

Door   i cannot allow your aperture
to my rented room   with light-blue air mattress
on the floor   single poster on the wall
sheep huddled in a copse
Door   clinically forensic   you collect fingerprints
is anybody in there
light careens off the sheep   explodes
all over the plaster
we know you're in there
Door   i shore up your handle
the watchman calls from the bell tower
il a sonné onze   il a sonné onze
my air mattress deflating   the room awash
in superwatted sheep   their blazing innards
we saw you go in there
Door   they are pounding you back to the sawmill
hold tight against the corridor   sheep inflame the room
i long for clicks   latches   a father's kiss goodnight
open up
Door   you are an earworm   i shall take the drubbing
open   close   do this in remembrance of me
ok we're coming in
Door   had all this not come between us
i would have allowed your thickened finger-hook
to hold my folds   my gathers
Door   i would have undressed for you

Katie Griffiths

Summer of 2015

That summer the beach by our house was half
empty and brashy. On the 5th of July we opposed

bailout terms with the shock of an earthquake
but the man of the house kept hammering

the piano like a cash register that wouldn't open.
Cracks appeared in highways and basements,

the last of our cured winter meat went rancid.
We stood in the doorway rattling a can

of drachmas against the widening background.
Still we drove the collision course

on the nerve of a poll and promises, lost
a game of chicken. And there was no

absence of queues outside banks, not only in Athens;
that summer waning under a car-crash moon.

At the Autoimmune Retreat

The farmhouse was strung in corpse vine,
the kitchen full of dead bodies.
Animal protein at every meal will stabilize
your cortisol levels, the facilitator chirped.
I bundled my shedding hair into a sheaf
and burnt it on the bonfire.
In the garden, roots were rotting
after autumn floods that followed
a summer of brushfires.
I walked the fields in a periwinkle crown,
thinking about my body changing
undeniably like the climate.
Lupus or rheumatoid arthritis?
The tests were inconclusive, but my biology
wouldn't speak ceasefire.
I googled the profession with the lowest
suicide rate, thought forward
to sleeping again as my temperature kindled.
At the breakfast buffet Christie joked,
We need year-round strawberries
like we need another wildfire.
I overwatered hydrangeas and orchids,
my joints tender, hair like the plastinated
nervous system at Body Worlds.
There was snow on the news
in a faraway country that wasn't snow
but rubble. I tucked into doughnuts
that make a tree of me, adding
each year another ring.
Great forests were being slashed
into fuelwood, the Congolese okapi dying.
These things happen.
Every friend on Instagram looked
ecstatic. Under cartoon clouds
of nitrogen we sprayed our bodies
with mosquito poison.

My thighs puckered and shook
as the earthquake-pleated city I come from.
Every contact leaves a trace.
Fingerprints are the small wounds
grooved when a baby touches the womb.
I deadheaded the garden,
each lovesick cricket stopped singing.
We talked about disease so much
the word undid itself.
On the last night, we bathed
in a light-grazed sky.

Adolescence

That year my flesh carried the fire.
A redback spider – god-dropped
into my chest – pulsed my heart.
I knew then my milk-laced days
were over. All my morning's music
clotted crimson-stark
and a web came spilling through
trapping the sun, its sky-old
summer buzz; so I stepped into it,
my adolescence fraying
into the evening's flameout.

Christmas in Paris

When she calls I leave the champagne
and oysters, go straight round. She opens
the door and I follow her into the cold

candlelit room. I've never seen him in a suit
in bed. Thinner, longer, he looks so serious.
I long to craze his halo of hair.

It's been three days, but I can't, she smooths
the pillow beside his, erupts with tears and sighs
then glares as if I'm unfeeling, shallow

breathing. But I'm thinking of the things
we shared, like air that's only for the living
and him lying between us, no longer a part.

Woodstock
after Jitish Kallat

Tomorrow I'm going back to Yasgur's farm.
Grass will be smoking, music flattening
trees, there'll be whale sound, cinnamon

candles, and a kohl-eyed girl in purple
kaftan, platform clogs, flowered peace-
band circling long hair, cross-legged

among beautiful people – half a million
strong. Are they accountants now? I turn
pages and pages of the battered journal,

even my writing has changed. Last week
at the Biennale I stood in a doorway, in words
projected on mist: *Become who you are*, but

just as songs rocked a town, I contain multitudes.
Tomorrow we're off to find one we left behind.

The Ambivalence of Doors

You and I were always coming and going
as if unsure which side of the door to choose.

We painted it blue, for abundance, for goodness,
blue to hinder insects, repel evil,

we threw salt, hammered horseshoes,
tried *haint* blue – *haint* as in haunt,

but restlessness remained.
After the war Janus barred his temple door

lest peace departed. Our peace departed.
We used Egyptian blue to honour

hieroglyphs and transitions,
the way no door should be opened

or closed without decision and respect.
I took to wearing blue mascara, shed blue tears,

our door couldn't help having two sides.
Behind it darkness grew

as if it was coated with the skin of monks.
I tapped on wood to scare any hidden presence.

Enter, come in, it whispered.
Exit, go without.

Acknowledgements

'Half-light' appeared in *Contemporary Poetry Series, Nature and Myth*, Corbel Stone Press, 2017.

'after you left' was shortlisted for the Bridport Prize 2022.

'Summer of 2015' was commended in the Oxford Brookes International Poetry Prize 2017 (EAL).

'At the Autoimmune Retreat' appeared in *AGNI*.

'Adolescence' was published in *Under the Radar*.

'Christmas in Paris', was published in *MIR Online*.

Biographies

Vasiliki Albedo is the winner of *Poetry International*'s summer 2021 chapbook competition and author of *Fire in the Oubliette* (Live Canon). Her poems have appeared or are forthcoming in *Poetry Review, Poetry London, Oxford Poetry* and elsewhere. She's been shortlisted for prizes including Aesthetica, Bridport and The Sylvia Plath Prize.

Hanne Busck-Nielsen is Danish and lives in the UK. Her poems, translations and reviews have appeared in magazines, anthologies and online. In 2015 she received the Special Commendation in Oxford Brookes University International Poetry Competition. Hanne was a finalist in the Cinnamon Press Pamphlet Competition, 2021.

Tom Cunliffe is an artist-writer who comes from Ellesmere Port. He studied Fine Art at Brighton. His work in both fields follows no particular line of enquiry. He is grateful for tripwires, potholes and banana skins. His pamphlet *Suit of Lights* (Pighog) was published in 2009. He lives in Seaford.

Beatriz Echeverri is originally from Colombia, where she worked as an architect/planner. London has been her home for many years. She is completing the Poetry School/Newcastle University MA in Writing Poetry. Beatriz has poems published in *The Alchemy Spoon* and in Tate Modern *Poetry from Art*, 2010/11, edited by Pascale Petit.

Katie Griffiths is British/Irish and grew up in Ottawa, Canada. Author of *The Attitudes* (Nine Arches Press, 2021) and *My Shrink is Pregnant* (Live Canon, 2019), she came second in 2018's National Poetry Competition and was in the first of the *Primers* series, also from Nine Arches Press.

Chris Hardy has travelled widely. After years in London, he now lives in Sussex. His poems have been published in magazines, anthologies, online, and been highly commended and shortlisted in the Poetry Society, Live Canon and other competitions. Chris's latest collection, *Key to the Highway,* is published by Shoestring Press.

Elizabeth Horsley divides her time between Greenwich and Cumbria. Her poems have been published in anthologies and a range of magazines including *The North*, *The Rialto*, *The Moth, Iota*, *Brittle Star* and *The Interpreter's House* and she has also reviewed for *The Alchemy Spoon.*

Mary Mulholland's poems have been published in journals and anthologies in both the UK and US, from *Arc* to *Under the Radar,* and had success in many competitions, most recently highly commended in The Rialto Nature & Place. Her debut pamphlet, *What the sheep taught me,* was published in 2022 by Live Canon.

Gillie Robic was born in India and lives in London. Besides being a poet, she is a voice artist and puppeteer in film, theatre and television. Widely published in magazines and anthologies, she has two collections, *Swimming Through Marble* and *Lightfalls*, from Live Canon, and a new pamphlet, *Open Skies,* in aid of Ukraine.

Lesley Sharpe's poems, reviews and essays appear in many journals and anthologies, as well as being short- and longlisted for several competitions including the Paper Swans Pamphlet Prize, The Rialto Nature & Place and Fish Poetry Prizes, The London Magazine Poetry Prize, Aesthetica, Cinnamon Debut Collection, Primers and Bridport.

Red Door Poets

Red Door Poets formed in 2015 after the founder members met when attending classes taught by Pascale Petit. As well as group meetings, they host regular online sessions via Zoom, alternating poetry readings with special guests and interviews with established poets.

https://www.facebook.com/reddoorpoets/
Twitter: @reddoorpoets
Instagram: reddoorpoets

Typesetting and Design Roger Bloor
Clayhanger Press
www.clayhangerpress.co.uk

Printed in Great Britain
by Amazon